GATHER THE GOOD

Written by Peggy Palmer
Illustrated by Rosemarie Gillen

Halo
PUBLISHING
INTERNATIONAL

ISBN: 978-1-61244-666-0
Library of Congress Control Number: 2018910166

Printed in the United States of America

Halo Publishing International
1100 NW Loop 410
Suite 700 - 176
San Antonio, Texas 78213
1-877-705-9647
www.halopublishing.com
contact@halopublishing.com

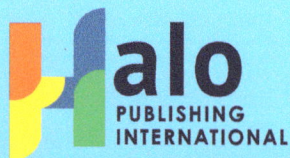

I am honored to lovingly dedicate this book to my treasures on earth who are my continual inspiration: Joe, Allyse, Tony, Dwayne and my extended family and friends.

A portion of the proceeds will directly benefit Peggy's Promise: out of my abundance, I will give.

JOY

LOVE

PATIENCE

HAPPY

4

"Mommy," said Ally, "why do you always tell me, Joey and Tony to gather the good?"

"We already know, so you don't have to say it every day… do you?"

"Well, sweetheart," Mom said, "every day is a new day, and we get the chance to decide what our day will give us!"

"If we decide what we gather to put in our hearts, it will be a better day."

"But Mom… We already know! I'm the youngest, and even I could show you how to be kind and gather the good, just like you taught us!" Ally said.

"We get to decide if we sit with a tablet in a dark room, watch TV and play video games all day…"

"Or we get to decide to go outside and experience the sunshine! If it's out, we lift our arms and soak in the sun!" said Ally.

"That's a great example of gathering the good." Mom said, "But what if it's raining?"

Ally said, "trick question, Mom. We need the rain too, and we can decide what the rain makes us feel! We can listen to the sounds to soothe us and help us relax. Right?"

"You got it!" Mom said, "can you tell me some of the good you've gathered since you woke up today?"

Ally counted on her fingers.

"One—Daddy stealing some of my yummy cereal and laughing with him!

Two—Smelling the toast just before it popped up.

Three—My brothers saying hi to the bus driver because she said hi first.

Four—The baby next door smiling at me.

Five—You sitting with me talking right now, eyeball to eyeball."

"I also waved at the grandpa who was walking across the street," said Ally. "It made my heart happy when he waved back and nodded his head. All those good things are gathered in my heart so when the clouds come out, I have plenty of sunshine in my pocket. This is fun!" Ally said as she skipped.

Mom pointed at the sky. "It's good to explore the clouds too, isn't it? Let's use our imaginations to see what's in the clouds today."

"I am thankful for the fluffy clouds. Are you?"

"Yes, they're pretty," said Ally, "I like when we lay in the grass for a minute and just look up."

"I'm so glad we can soak in the sun, enjoy the sounds of the rain and explore the clouds. We need them all," said Mom.

Mom glanced at her watch. "Let's go meet the boys at the bus stop!"

"Yeah!" Ally clapped. "The boys will like that! Dad says just showing up for our family is important and makes you feel good. I'll ask the questions today, Mom. Just watch me. I know I can do it!"

The big yellow bus pulled up to the curb, and her brothers stepped off. Questions rolled off Ally's tongue before the bus even pulled away. "Hi, Joey and Tony! Did you give and collect smiles? Were you kind? Who was your favorite friend? Did you help someone? What are you thankful for? Who was nice to you at school today?

"Sheesh," Joey said. "Are you going to let us answer?"

Ally laughed. "Oops... yes!

"I am thankful that you and mom came to walk with us. I was helpful to my teacher. I was honest about not finishing my homework. Bobby was my favorite friend, and I'm hungry," said Joey. "Let's hurry home, so I can get a snack! Does that about cover it?"

"Ahem..." Tony looked at his brother. "Anyone kind to you?"

"Yes," said Joey. "My brother helped me remember my jacket from the bus."

Tony crouched down beside Ally. "How was your day, munchkin?"

"Good! I learned that mommy needs to tell us things every day even if we know them. Cause every day we get to tell our brains what to do! And if we gather the good, we'll be good hearted people. And that's better for us AND the people we love." Ally said without stopping for a breath.

"Yep!" Tony high-fived Ally. "That's what we all learned at your age. We all need to be able to gather the good when we go to school. Sometimes it's a hard day, and people around us are cranky. But we decide what vibes we put out. Nobody can decide for us."

It's our choice every day!

"We need the sun, the rain and the clouds. And we can gather the good everywhere we go even if there's yucky stuff around," said Ally.

"Yes!" Mom nodded and put her arm around Ally. "We focus our gaze to the good because it's our choice every day!"

"Right," said Joey, throwing his jacket over his shoulder. "Some kids just don't think about it. They just look around and collect everything. WE can help a friend smile when they're down, but we don't need to collect their frown to take home with us!"

"I like that you're thinking about the positive things in your day. Knowing that we can tell our brains what to focus on is a lesson even some parents are still working on," said Mom. "Good job, kids, I'm proud of you all!"

Ally threw back her shoulders and stood tall. "I'm proud I can always remember to gather the good in my heart!"

GATHER THE GOOD

www.ingramcontent.com/pod-product-compliance
Lightning Source LLC
LaVergne TN
LVHW070839080426
835511LV00025B/3482